# WHEN YOUR HUSBAND HAS DIED

## A Survival Guide

### CORINNE EDWARDS

# DEDICATION

*A few years ago, I wrote an article for my blog called,*

*When Your Husband Has Died – A survival guide.*

*Over 3000 women, from all over the world, found it and started commenting.*

*They shared their pain, their experiences, sadness, success, but most of all – understood, supported and loved each other.*

*This book is dedicated to those dear ones I have grown to love.*

# *Gone*

He is gone.

Only a wisp of his presence remains.
An unfinished life,
the look of wonderment on his face
when he first held his son,
pipes on a shelf,
cuff links from Italy,
a family laughing by a Christmas tree.

They shipped his things from the
office.
Forty years in a small box.

It was a transitory joining,
the years, an instant in time.

At the end,
I tried to heal for him,
make it right, stop the pain,
do it for him, carry him.
but he carried his,
and I carry mine.

He is memories.
A dark blue Lincoln.
Begonias in the basement for the
winter.
Japanese fish in a pond.
*September Song.*

he is gone

# INTRODUCTION

The funeral was over. It was beautiful. Everyone said so. I think my husband would have been pleased.

Everyone had been so kind and supportive. The house full of loving people, food being delivered and family and friends so willing to help in any way.

My husband had been ill for five long years and the end was terrible. He had gone from about 200 pounds down to 70 pounds and was living in pain in spite of morphine and a cocktail of many narcotics.

During the last week of his life I was praying that God would take him. So, when he died, at home, with all the family around him, I was grateful that it was peaceful and finally over for him.

All I felt is relief. I had already grieved for five years and I thought that was the end of it. I didn't know it was a new beginning.

Those well-meaning people who arrived to support me had lots of advice.

Perhaps, you received the same -

*IT'S A BLESSING*

*LIFE GOES ON*

*TIME HEALS*

*YOU ARE STRONGER THAN YOU
KNOW*

*THANK GOD YOU HAVE CHILDREN*

*YOU WILL PULL YOURSELF
TOGETHER*

*HE'S NOT SUFFERING ANY MORE*

*YOU HAVE TO GET OUT MORE*

And the religious ones added –

GOD WILL SUPPORT YOU

GET YOUR SPIRITUAL LIFE IN
ORDER

IT IS GOD'S WILL

JESUS NEEDED HIM IN HEAVEN
(WHY?)

> BUT WHAT DO YOU DO
> TONIGHT?

And for the rest of your time on this
earth.  Your life has changed forever.

It was time to hear from a widow.
Someone who knows where you are.

And more important,

WHAT LIES AHEAD FOR YOU?
WHERE DO YOU START?

What is needed is a book for widows
by a widow.

This is that book. I wrote it for you.

# CHAPTER ONE – STARTING OVER

If your husband died suddenly, you had a different scenario from mine.

You were probably living in such a state of shock and disbelief that you felt nothing at all for a long time.

But, I can only write from my own background. As time goes forward, we will start to share many of the same experiences.

It took a while until I started to realize how many things my husband took care of. Repairs, stocks, the bills, ANYTHING to do with cars –

I was driving home from shopping when I heard a siren behind me. It was a police car. He came to the window of my car.

You just made an illegal left turn. Didn't you see that sign?

*No, I'm sorry, officer, I didn't.*

That sign is as big as a house, lady. You women drivers!

*I'm sorry. I didn't see it.*

Do you know your license plate expired four months ago?

*No.*
And your city sticker expired two months ago?

*No. I didn't realize it.*

What is it with you, lady? Do you know I'm going to have to give you three tickets? Why didn't you take care of these things?

*Men do these things with cars. I'm sorry, but my husband died. He always took care of the cars.*

Well, I'm sorry to hear about your husband, but you're the one who is going to have to show up in court. You're going to have to get it together, lady.

*Okay. I will.*

Look, this is none of my business, but I notice these things. According to the sticker on your car, you haven't changed the oil in 10,000 miles. You should take care of that.

*Thanks for telling me. I will.*

And start looking at signs.

*Okay.*

He gave me the tickets but there was a sweetness, a caring in the way that gruff policeman told me to change my oil – a cop doing his job with kindness. It was an expensive experience but oddly comforting. And he was right.

This lady had to get it together!

I wasn't ready yet.

# CHAPTER TWO – CHANGES

At first, I had a lot of attention from friends. I was included in activities just as I had when I was married.

Then, slowly, it started to change. I was still invited to the big parties but not to the dinner parties or the pizza on Friday nights. That seemed to be just for couples. I still had a relationship with the "girls" for lunch and I spent time with my kids but it left many evenings open.

The absence of the stress and medical crisis I had shared with my husband for years had left this big void – a big empty space. I tried to remember what occupied my time before it all happened. I realized for the first time that this is a couple's world.

Going to a wedding or a big occasion was torture. There you are all dressed up sitting alone at an empty table with no one asking you to dance.

Did you get a lot more advice now? I did.

"When are you going to sell the house? It's too big for you."

"Life goes on you know.

You're still attractive. Get out there and find someone."

"Watch out for the gold-diggers. They are looking for someone like you."

"Get involved in some activities. You'll meet some new people."

"You should join a widow's support group.""Have you thought about working at something different? It would be good for you to get out."

"You should travel more. Get out there."

Everything seemed to have something to do about getting out. I owned a travel agency at the time so I did have a job.

But I found myself longing to go home to my big chair in the living room. I thought about that chair all day. It was a safe place. And I didn't want to travel alone.

After a few months as a recluse in my house, I thought maybe I should venture out a little. Suppose they were all right?

## CHAPTER THREE – GETTING OUT

They told me I should get out more,
see new people.
I'd never meet anyone
sitting in the house.

So I thought
I'd try it—
but I'll go alone.
In case I hate it,
I can just go home.

I bought a ticket
to a Beethoven concert.
The music was beautiful
and I realized I had to quit smoking,
not for health reasons.
Standing alone at intermission
having a cigarette
is terrifying.

So I just went home.

Signed up for a class in tarot.

Each student at the table
had a crystal (don't touch it!)
as big as a fist.
The instructor had three.

Before I found a crystal
that spoke to me,

I just went home.

There was the Over-Forty Singles
Club.
An elderly man asked me to dance,
which surprised me.
I saw him come in.
He could hardly walk.

He was concealing an erection
that would have shamed a twenty-year-
old.

I just went home.

Went to a town board meeting.
There was a motion on the floor
to buy the police department a
coffeepot.

After it was seconded and passed,
they argued for an hour.

Before I bought the cops a pot,

I just went home.

At the Consciousness Raising Center,
a good place to meet interesting people,
I was assigned to a group
to explore protections from spirit entity
invaders.

I didn't know they were out,
and before one of them invaded me,

I just went home.

Visited a widows support group.
They cried a lot.
The lecture for the evening was on how
to write a check,
and the mystery of the bank statement.
Before I started to feel too superior,

I just went home.

At the Council on Foreign Relations,
a fat banker from Citicorp
mesmerized the audience with
information
on a South American monetary crisis.
Before I announced it had been in all
the papers,

I just went home.

Obviously, I have not found my niche
yet.

## CHAPTER FOUR – THE ART OF DOING NOTHING

I wasn't ready to get out.

But, most of us go to bed at night with the same thought.

"Now – what did I do today that was productive?"

It is as though we have to justify our being on the planet by doing – doing – doing. Busy – busy – busy.

What's wrong with doing nothing?

Nothing.

Can we stand the guilt?

What's wrong with -

Putting on the TV to On-Demand and watching reruns of *Sex and the City* or old movies. Getting around to all those *Saturday Reviews* piled up next to your chair and leisurely reading them.

Is it a sin if –

You do not check your email. (Well, maybe once at the end of the day) You do not answer the phone. You have caller ID and voice mail so you can just see if it is someone who may have an emergency but if they do they will call you back ten times until you answer.

It is your life.  You are recovering from a war.

You have post traumatic stress disorder.  You need quiet time  -

To think without any interruptions.  To mourn.

You can experience "A-hah" moments and get new ideas because there is nothing intruding on your thoughts. Nobody is gobbling up your mind with their demands and problems. You are spending time with your most important person. Yourself.

You can make decisions for the world. Well, maybe not the world but you can decide if you should buy a new couch or a dishwasher.

This time belongs to you. You are your own most important priority.

The reason that we find it so hard to allow free time for ourselves is tied up in our self-worth. Deep down, we really don't think we deserve it. I would love to know where that came from. Who instilled that crazy ethic that we cannot be idle? Deepak Chopra, the famous author, says we are "not human beings we are human doings."

It is also about control. I had a friend who suggested that we should form a 10-step Control Anonymous group. Somehow, we feel if we let down for one minute the world will not go on without our input. Our business and our families will just fall apart.

And yet, there have been times when we've had the flu and we were laid up for a week and somehow life just continued to tick on and things got done later that were urgent.

My late husband had the theory down. He was a stockbroker and he took a month off in the winter every year. When his clients protested he would say, "Look, pretend I just had a heart attack. You'd be very sympathetic. This is my yearly heart attack." He never lost a client. They survived with his assistant during that month. He has been gone from this world for years now.

Why did it take me so long to learn from him?

How long is it going to take you?

## CHAPTER FIVE – YOU'LL NEVER GET OVER IT

.The day after my husband died, a friend came to see me. His wife had been killed by a drunk driver.

His words were a surprise. They did not sink in until much later.

*"You will never get over this. If you know this in advance, you won't try. You will not struggle and condemn yourself for not succeeding."*

He was right. His words became a consolation. I stopped trying.

There is a thread among widows that says that they will recover from the overwhelming grief and their life will become normal again.

That is why I decided to write this book. I wanted to share my friend's words with you.

The old normal is gone. There is a hole in your heart and your being that will never be filled.

A psychic told me that those who have gone on to the other side are allowed to stay around for a while. To help and comfort. But not forever. I thought I felt my husband's presence. But then, less and less.  Dreaming of him only once in a while.  But , everyday, he has never left my heart.

After a period of intense pain, you will be different.  The person you were is gone.  It is an amputation.  Eventually, a new person will emerge.  It will be the new normal.

A new life will start to happen but the limb you have lost will not grow back.  You will have something in common with a soldier who bravely runs a marathon despite having a prosthesis for a leg.

As my friend said, you will never get over it.

This new person will have a life which includes peace, love  and even laughter, community and new friendships.  It can and will happen in your own time.

I believe there is a tiny gift inherent in every unspeakable tragedy.

One is compassion.  I could not have written that article for widows if I had not experienced the grief of loss in my life.  I would not have been able to connect.

Another is knowing how to help someone else who is in that state of extreme pain.

The world does not allow you much time. As though others can replace the one you have lost. I find you get about two months to get over it. With all fairness, they don't know what to say. What they don't know is that they need only to listen.

Part of the gift is giving someone else your time to listen far beyond the window allowed. You know they have no one to talk to. You reach out more.

The sharing of this gift, when you are able, will comfort you.

You will no longer struggle to "get over it." You will trust that if you are still on this earth, there must be a reason.

The new normal person will find that reason. It may not quite exist yet - but it is becoming.

## CHAPTER SIX – MEN – AND MONEY

The thing that surprised me the most was the pressure from well-meaning friends, clients and family - to replace my husband- to find a man   almost immediately.

I admit I thought about it. But the thought of "dating" was alien to me. Never mind finding one but what do you say to a date? I hadn't had a date in years.

And what do you do with your wedding ring? When are you supposed to take it off? My ideal situation would be to find a person exactly like my husband who would be deposited on my doorstep by helicopter. To go back to my old, comfortable life.

Back to where my husband was well.

You might get the opposite pressure from your kids or your heirs. They tend to build shrines to your saintly husband. They might be horrified if you mentioned the idea of another man in your life even if there is no one in sight.

I've talked to a lot of widows about this and I hate to tell you this but it is about the MONEY. Their inheritance.

They have seen stories on TV about scams. The nice and smart women who have been fleeced by con men.

You have to assure your heirs that you are not stupid. That you are reworking all your financial matters to coincide with your new status as a single woman. And you will keep them informed of what you are doing.

And as the cop said, you have to get it together, lady.

It's an unpleasant task because the process brings us in contact with our own mortality. We all have this little secret. Everyone is going to die except us so there is no rush.

I started with conversations with my children. I wanted to know, of the few valuable things in my home, which they would want to inherit. You need to have that information when you make a new will.

And then, find out exactly what assets you have. Your husband may have handled all these things. I know mine did. If he had an accountant who did his taxes, that would be your first step. Otherwise, you will have to dig through his records.

The next is to find an attorney who specializes in wills and trusts. Not your friend who does real estate closings. A will is not enough. You will need a Revocable Living Trust.

A lot of people are afraid of a trust because they think they will lose control of their money and their house. No. You are the executor and you can do whatever you want. Sell the house. Buy a condo. Trade your stocks.

Next would be to find someone to invest the money you have.

You will be surprised at who will approach you on doing this for you. But do not give your money to your brother-in-law's cousin's son who sells annuities and promises you an income for life. At least, not until you do some big research. You want to deal with a large firm and with a broker who knows what he is doing.

Don't start being a day trader yourself to save commissions. Probably, you don't know what you are doing.

Look for a broker who is a Certified Financial Planner. I was lucky. My son is a CFP with Merrill Lynch. I know from that how hard he had to work to get that designation. It is the Mercedes of broker levels and involves many classes, tests and experience. They are trained to look at your whole picture and will work with your accountant and attorney. Talk to a few and decide who you like.

Tell your heirs what you have done. Even offer to show them all your documents. They will stop worrying about you and someone stealing you blind.

So much for someone who went through this process. It is not pleasant but when it is done it is done.

After you have signed all the papers, you will feel a little better.

This is the first step of many – where you will come to terms that you are alone.

Looking forward.

Not holding on to the past.

## CHAPTER SEVEN - HOLDING ON TO THE PAST

Holding on to the past is trying to breathe life into a play which is closed. It is struggling to raise the curtain in a dark theatre, on a dusty stage, by ourselves.

The main player – your husband is gone.

The stage in empty.

It is going over our everyone's lines, long since said, playing all the parts – alone. It is being stuck.

It is entrapment in a time warp. The costumes no longer fit. The buttons have popped. We are different people today but we still force the action.

It is a brutal attack on ourselves, because we become, on this stage, both the victim and the attacker.

Jerry Jampolsky, author of *Love Is Letting Go of Fear*, says that "Forgiveness is giving up all hope of a better past."

We don't forgive ourselves. We get caught in the "if onlies," hanging on to dreams which did not come true, the terrible loss of a beloved who has died

—

We even go further back with our regrets –

A loss brings back earlier losses.

A unhappy childhood, an old love affair which did not end happily ever after, a youth gone – opportunities which have disappeared.

The game is over, but we are bad sports. We refuse to accept defeat. We run the tape over and over. We can put it on rewind but we can't get into the movie anymore.

Dr. Wayne Dyer, author of many wonderful books, likens it to our holding on to the bars of a cage. We rattle them, desperately trying to get free. But the bars are just in front of us. If we look to the right, to the left or behind us, there are no bars.

All we have to do is turn around and walk away.

We are looking for love in that past. A cry that was not answered, a happy childhood, that lover who left, that job to validate us. We wanted to feel safe, wanted, worthwhile.

Yet we know that we cannot infuse love into what is gone. We can only give and receive love now.

We have shackled ourselves in bondage. It is time to walk away from the cage.

The past is not holding us. We are holding it.

Picture all your past relationships, even you treasured husband –

Now lifeless energy forms, hanging on hooks in a closet. The closet goes with you wherever you go.

The relationships are part of you – they have made up your experience – but you are no longer part of them. Although you carry them with you, you can no longer breathe life into them. They are your past.

You can open the closet door and look at the array. But, if you take them out and try to carry them around, they are a heavy and unnecessary burden.

You travel with your closet, filling it more and more each day. But it is carried for you. There is no need for you to put it on your back.

You cannot lose it because it is the summation of who you are.

But it no longer applies to your present except as memories, experience and learning.

These are the records of your life and of your heart. It is up to you to decide to keep the door closed, or to live within the boundaries of a closet.

We can't put the past on rewind. The buttons are stuck. The actors have gone on to other roles. The set has been dismantled.

That old movie is over.

You are writing a new script.

## CHAPTER EIGHT – THE PAINFUL STUFF

One of the most painful things to face is your husband's clothes still hanging in the closet – or a coat on a hook behind the door – and his shoes.

You've offered his things to your family and they have selected what they want.

There is still a lot left.

It feels so final. It is usually the last thing we want to face.

It was bad when we received that check from the insurance company. Would they pay if he was alive? No. That was hard.

But somehow – this is the hardest. The last straw.

Consciously, we know he won't be wearing those things. And there a few we should probably keep.

One friend told me she wore her husband's pajamas every night. It's OK.

One of the ways I found peace is to remind myself, in this bad economy, that there is someone who would be happy to have a warm coat or a presentable suit to look for a job.  We forget that in our grief to hold on.

My Polish cleaning woman asked if she could have my husband's shoes.

*"But, there are so many.  Who would they fit?"*

She looked amazed – "They have few shoes.  The size does not matter."

I think my husband would like the idea of all his shoes walking around in a tiny village in Poland.

I kept his slippers.

## CHAPTER EIGHT – CHILDREN

*Alie, are you in there?*

Yes.

*Would you come out a minute? I want to talk to you.*

What do you want?

*Look, I want to apologize for what I said. I realize that you meant well when you told me that you were paying all the bills in the house from now on. It was mean of me to say that you could pay the bills when you bring in the money. I'm just under a lot of stress. I'm not myself lately.*

I thought it would help you if I did what Dad did.

*I know, Alie. But, there's plenty of time for you to have those responsibilities in the future. But not now. You don't have to pay the bills. I can do it.*

I wouldn't mind doing it.

*I know you wouldn't. But it isn't necessary.*

*And another thing, Alie. I don't want you to think you have to stay home and*

*keep me company. I want you to go out
with your friends like you always have.*

I don't want you to be alone, Mom.

*Please, Alie. I want you to be a kid.
Just be a kid. That would help me the
most. I'm doing fine. Just be a kid.
Please.*

*And I'm very sorry I spoke to you that
way.*

I love you, Mom.

*I know. And I love you. Very much*

## CHAPTER NINE - GROWING OLDER – BEING A GOOD SPORT

*We are always the same age inside.*
**Gertrude Stein**

Your birthday is coming up or has just past. Maybe it is a big number ending with a zero or a five. Those are the toughest ones. The others in between seem to slide by like they haven't happened.

You are in good health and are taking care of yourself but the scary part is when you look at the Obituaries in the paper there are now names you recognize. You probably never even looked before.

Not only have you lost your husband but a good friend has died.

A couple have developed sicknesses. Bad ones.

The reason that social security is in trouble is that they never expected so many to live past 65 – long enough to collect the benefits. Not true anymore.

Here are a few suggestions that you might consider to weather this storm. They follow the five stages of grief that Elizabeth Kubler Ross made famous. In a way, getting older is a form of grief

1. DENIAL. Of course, the first thing is you start lying about your age. (Someone once told me you have to start lying by at least five years because everyone else is lying and they immediately add five years on to what you claim is your age)

It doesn't help you because you know the truth and you are the one who is being affected. So, my first suggestion is to tell the truth because you are then admitting it to yourself. You don't have to shout it to the treetops, but if it comes up, tell the truth. That is the beginning of freedom. You will probably be surprised because instead of someone feeling sorry for you because you are SO OLD, you will probably hear, "You have got to be kidding! You look great!" And it gives other people confidence that they will live as long and look as good as you do. It's a public service.

2. ANGER. I haven't done —- (Fill in your grievances here) Then, get a yellow pad and get really mad about what you think you have missed. Include your petty illness, your aches and pains and the fact that your body looks terrible. Don't leave anything out you have missed and feel you may never do. Include things like you don't have quite the energy you used to have. Get it all out. Remember, no one else

will see this list but you and there is relief in admitting all to yourself. Awareness of any problem is the first step in healing.

3. BARGAINING. Please God let me live long enough to (again your list)

Decide you will.

When I was in the travel business, I had a client who owned a funeral parlor. He used to book a big trip between Thanksgiving and Christmas. He called it his "slow season." I was curious about it because it was also flu season. Didn't a lot of people die then? He told me people who make it past the first holiday do not die because they decide not to. So decide you will live long enough for your bargain to manifest. Chances are you will, even if your wish is several years away. The Power of Intention is truly powerful!

4. DEPRESSION. You may need some medical help with this. Do not be ashamed to talk to your doctor. A round of anti-depressants might give you a lift so you can get on with the life you have left. It is very hard to reinvent yourself if you are depressed.

And, literally, this is your next step. One of the hardest parts of getting older is not having a goal, a passion.

We are very ready to say, what's the use?"

The "use" is that we have learned a lot. We have made mistakes. We have had successes.

There are young people out there who need to know what we know – including your children and grandchildren. They are hungry for your guidance and your experience.

There are small businesses that are struggling and you have gone through it. There are organizations like the Girls and Boys Club who could use you to help kids who have no responsible parents who need your wisdom and help with their homework.

You may say you don't have the energy. You may have to push yourself to volunteer once a week but you will feel better about it after that day. And you won't feel so lonely.

You owe the planet something by taking up all that space for so many years. It is time to pay your bills. Do you think that someone who needs help is going to say, "Thanks, but you are too old?" No way.

5. ACCEPTANCE. We all have this little secret. Everyone else is going to

die except us. So, this is the toughest one.

Chances are that we have a number of years to go before we go. But what has to be faced is that this is the downhill side of the slope now.

And when it is time to say goodbye to this world, please God, let us be grateful for the opportunities this life has given us. It has been a wild and wonderful ride!

But if you are reading this, you are still alive. And, if you are still alive, it means that there is a reason for it. It is up to each of us to decide that reason.

And help us to go on gracefully to whatever is next.

## CHAPTER TEN – MOVING ON

There was a group of women I started to meet.  I didn't know about them until now.

They actually got theatre and symphony tickets and went without a man.

We had dinner together.  Sometimes, just met for a drink after work. I had company. It was nice and filled in some of the gaps in my life.

I found out that I would not die if I went to a movie alone.

 I still missed my old friends and my old life but what they say about time healing is true.  I started to "get it together."

I met some new widows. It's a private club you never wanted to join but suddenly I became the authority on how to get through this period of suddenly being alone with the newer ones. I had put some time in.

It made me realize how little help there is out there for us. We are the silent victims of life. People do not want to be reminded that this could also happen to them.

A couple of them had also made it through a year or two.

At first, the thought of another man in our lives had been disgusting. When people brought it up it was so foreign.

But a couple of them had started some tentative dating. They actually went on Internet dating sites.

They found that there are lonely men out there. Nice people. They were scared just like us. Many were widowed or divorced and were looking for company.

Not necessarily marriage – but someone to join for dinner – to do some fun things together.

Perhaps they had children close to your children's ages. It might be nice.

I started thinking about it.

### BUT HOW DO YOU DO THIS?

Hold on to your hat. I am going to give you a short course.

If you are not ready yet, save this for later.

## CHAPTER ELEVEN - INTERNET DATING – A DRIVER'S MANUAL

How do you start dating when you are now a widow?

Recent widows are in such a state of deep grief that every artery is open. The thought of dating is foreign to them. They are just trying to get through the day.

But I have noticed lately that some of us who have been alone for a couple of years are tentatively thinking about dating.

Asking for advice and they are scared to death.

I am writing this especially for them. And maybe, for you.

Please note, my dear ones, I am not suggesting you start dating if you are not interested or ready. This is for the ones who have asked for information.

The rest of you can eavesdrop if you like. If you are recently widowed, you might learn something here.

It is scary putting yourself out there. What is no one answers? You worry that you are not gorgeous and visualize yourself as not good enough that anyone would be interested in you.

Maybe it is better to just accept your fate and not take a chance of being rejected even if you are lonely and wanting some company with a nice man.

It could be an opportunity for you to do a little makeover on yourself. You've been through a rough time.

 Is it time to spruce up your wardrobe with a few pretty casual outfits? Maybe a new hair style and a session with a makeup artist at your local department store?

 If nothing else, it could cheer you up. You have forgotten how attractive you are, inside and out.

Let's look together at a few things.

This comes up a lot.

**You are not being unfaithful to your late husband.  He was a wonderful person. Would he resent your having a companion now that he is gone? He would want you to have some happiness.**

Get that out of the way

The people out there who might answer your ad are not all George Clooney.

Time has scribbled unkindly on many of the faces. Some are overweight, be speckled, have some health problems, and are not all rich guys looking for a Playboy bunny. They are as scared and lonely as you are.

Let's not jump into the deep end of the pool yet.

I'd like you to sit down first and list all your good points and likes and dislikes.

Do you have a good sense of humor? Do you like music? What kind? Are you into politics? Do you like to travel? Where? What are you longing to see in the world? Are you a good cook? Do you like certain types of foods?

Do you consider yourself attractive? Have a close friend help you with this. It is hard to evaluate ourselves.

This could be a good exercise for you whether you are thinking of dating or not.

You have thought of yourself as a twosome for so long that you have forgotten you have an identity of your own.

Think now in terms of "I" or "me" – not we. No rush. Take your time.

**Now, let's describe the kind of man you might enjoy spending some time with.**

What is important to you? Not necessarily looks, although that could be an item.

If you are tall, you might want a tall man. If you are religious, you might want someone of your own religion.

General characteristics. Probably some of the ones your late husband had that you especially liked. What about ethnicity? Race? Age? Be honest. No one is going to see this list but you.

You might want to state your preference for a widower. Some divorced men are very bitter (and broke) and will bore you to tears telling you about their ex.

The reason I am suggesting these practice sessions is that you will have to answer two very important questions if you should decide to go ahead and start looking on personal Internet sites.

**The first is "Tell us about yourself."**

**The second is "How would you describe the person you are seeking?"**

Practice writing each of these answers. Be truthful.

Are you still with me?

The next question which will be asked is your age. My experience is that everyone is lying – some a little. Some a lot. Most by about five years.

People search on the sites in segments. Like 30 to 40, 40 to 50, 50 to 60 etc. So if you are 41, you might list yourself as 39 so you fit in the lower category. You can fess up later.

**You will need a picture. No one will answer if you don't post it. Make it a fairly recent one. One where you look friendly. It does not have to be a glamour shot.**

You will have to download the picture into your computer in order to post it on an Internet dating site. If you don't know how to do it, get some help.

I can feel you backing up. Now other people will know, right?

No. No one is going to pay $30.00 a month for a minimum of three months to snoop on you. The people on these sites are looking or they would not be there.

Which brings up another point.

DON'T TELL ANYONE EXCEPT
MAYBE YOUR BEST FRIEND YOU
ARE DOING THIS.

Everyone else will have something to
say about it. This is your experiment.

Now to choose which site to join.

Match.com is the biggest – all ages.
All religions.

Or J-Date if you are Jewish and would
consider dating no one else.

My impression that E-Harmony is good
if you are in your 30's.

Otherwise, pick a big site. You will
have more selection and find people
who are more geographically suitable.

Take a deep breath and sign up.

You don't have to put your profile up
right away. You are now a member
and you can look around to see who is
there. Look at both men and women in
your age group. You can read other's
descriptions before you post your own
information.

How does your introduction sound in
comparison and the person you are
seeking?

Take the plunge.  You can change anything later.

Answer the questions.

Some are silly.  Like "What would you consider a good first date?"

People will contact you if they are interested.  You can then decide if you are.  Ignore the ones that don't appeal to you.

Remember, no one knows who you are. All contact with a prospect will be through the site.  Not your personal email.

Remember you can contact people too.

If you find someone – don't give too much information.  Never your personal email.   God forbid, your phone or exact location.  Keep it light.

If you decide to get in touch with someone – get their telephone number. Block your number when YOU call THEM.

Have several conversations before you decide to meet.

**The next question that comes up is "How do I check these people out?"**

Hard to do at first but there are safety measures you can take

Arrange to meet in a public place like a library or a coffee shop.

Drive your own car.

Don't tie up your time by arranging to have dinner. Or, even lunch. You might decide right away this person is not for you and then you are stuck for possibly hours. Meeting for the first time should be short, like a cup of coffee. You will know.

Keep up these precautions until you feel comfortable that he is just a nice man looking for companionship like you. Any decent guy will understand.

Tell your best friend where you are going and when and the man's telephone number.

Don't give out much personal information. You ask the questions. Most people love to talk about themselves so they will be happy to have the opportunity.

There are a few ways you can check on someone. If he has a business card, call the number and ask the operator his exact title because your boss wants to write to him and you want it get it right.

If he does not work there – forget it.

If he is never available on a weekend, he either married or has a steady girlfriend. Skip that one.

Stay away from the ones who say they are "separated." It's usually a mess. Tell them to get back to you when they are free if they appeal to you.

If he happens to have a land line, go to 411.com and look for reverse search. Cell phones are harder to check.

And don't forget running his name on Google. Big Brother has information on all of us. You might be surprised how much you can find out about everyone.

I am not telling you these things to scare you. – the great majority of men are exactly who they say they are.

The only unpleasant experience I ever had was with a charming man who seemed unable to speak about his late wife, even after a second date. I figured he was in too much grief.

When I pressed him, turned out he was married. When I protested, he said, "But my wife will love you."

I just left. Please. Threesomes are not my thing.

So, what do you think? Are you ready to try it? If not, that's OK.

Now you have an Official Driver's Manual.

Maybe next year. Or, sometime.

Internet dating can be a lot of fun.  An adventure.

When you are ready.

Only you can decide.

## CHAPTER TWELVE - SOME LAST WORDS

How many times have you heard this?

**"When are you going to sell that house?  It's too big for you."**

Please.  If you can afford it – WAIT.

It's the worst time to sell – and besides – do you know how much STUFF you have?

Few things will fit in a small place or your big pieces will be out of scale.

I stayed in my five bedroom house for five years.  I blamed it on my 11 year old Doberman.  The vet said it would be hard for him to adjust.

It's also nice to have all that room in a house if your kids come to visit.

Then, I moved to downtown Chicago.

It is true that it is expensive to keep up your place.  But if you move to a condo, you will have maintenance fees.  Add those up.

Those fees were $400. a month when I moved in and in four years went up to$800.  Buildings need  fixing.

And I had to get dressed to go down to pick up the mail. It felt like I was living in a hotel.

I moved again. To a more reasonable town house out of the center of the city. I like it. It feels like a smaller version of my big house.

Take your time. Do your research. Do it slowly. You probably will make a change but don't rush if you don't have to.

You don't need any more drastic changes.

**The other questions I hear is when you should take off your wedding rings.**

That is also an individual decision. Maybe you won't.

If you are dating, leave them home. It is a turn off.

I have friends who decided to convert them to a new ring. Redesigned them. They are beautiful and they would like to keep them and enjoy them. Or make them into a pendant. There are many ways to remember your beautiful marriage.

Some women pass them down to a daughter who is getting married. Usually, she will treasure it.

I don't have daughters. My ring belonged to my grandmother. I gifted it to my favorite niece. She was thrilled. It will stay in the family.

**There is a rumor that it takes you a year to get over a death. Where that information comes from I have no idea.**

It is true that the first year is the hardest. All those "firsts" to get through. Anniversaries. Birthdays. Holidays.

The anticipation of the date is worse than when the date arrives. Somehow, you get through it. But those dates never leave you.

I feel it takes as long as it takes before you even get to a point of feeling normal – whatever that means – again. I don't think you ever get over a great loss – but you somehow re-invent yourself as you go along.

Don't let anyone rush you. Things will get better. But in your own time frame.

The most important thing to remember is that this is your life. There are many decisions to make in this new world you are living.

Make sure YOU are the one who is making them.

## AN INVITATION

*A miracle is never lost. It may touch many people you have never even met, and produced undreamed of changes in situations of which you are not even aware.*

*A Course in Miracles*

You never know where your words will go.

A few years ago, I wrote an article on my blog called *When Your Husband Has Died – A Survival Guide.* It is that article that inspired this book.

I expected some widows would find it but I didn't know how since I had so few readers at the time.

But they did.

It has become my most read post. To date, there are over 3000 comments. From widows in their twenties with small children to women in their 80's.

They come from all over the world. Most use just their first names.

It reminds me that every action has a reaction – and often one that you never expected. That article feels like an accidental miracle to me.

It is now no longer my article.  It has become a forum and belongs to everyone.  The women tell their stories and share their challenges – and they encourage each other with comfort and advice.

The early commentators keep coming back and update the others with their progress.  Many mention that it is a place they can talk freely since no one knows who they are or where they live.  They can share without burdening their families and friends.

Please join us.

Just copy and paste this link into your search browser.

http://www.personal-growth-with-corinne-edwards.com/when-your-husband-has-died-a-survival-guide/

You will have to put in your email address, because that is the way blogs work, but no one sees that but me.  And I will never share your information .

This could be your accidental miracle today.

Pour yourself a cup of coffee and come on over.

 We are waiting to meet you.

Get up

Get up

The universe is dancing.

You must get up and dance!

you don't have a choice

if you can't hear the song

and you fall out of step

it will drag you along.

Get up!

Get up!

The universe is dancing!

You must get up and dance!

though your heart weighs you down

like a full term child,

your grief has stunned your mind,

and you slip in the flood

of your bloody tears,

you cannot stay behind.

Get up! Get up!

THE UNIVERSE IS DANCING!

YOU MUST GET UP AND DANCE!

It's dancing and dancing and dancing
and dancing

GET UP!

# ABOUT THE AUTHOR

Corinne Edwards has traveled several life paths - from business owner to sales trainer, author, lecturer, poet, TV producer, blogger and media coach.

She is the author of *Low Pain Threshold, Love Waits on Welcome, Reflections from a Woman Alone, A Woman Without A Man, Sales, Lies and Naked Truths* and *When Your Husband Has Died – A Survival Guide.*
.

She produced/hosted *Book Tours.., with Corinne Edwards* for *Wisdom Television* on national cable.

In recent years, her focus has shifted to the area of personal growth and human potential. Corinne has conducted self esteem classes based on the principals of love and forgiveness in A Course in Miracles in Cook County Jail. Her program for rehabilitation for prostitutes was one of the first of its kind in the country.

Currently, her burning passion is blogging on her site http://www.personal-growth-with-corinne-edwards.com

This book was expanded from an article on that site, by the same name.

Over 3000 widows have posted their stories anonymously to that article.

Those women inspired her to write this book for widows – by a widow. Her intention is there are few practical guides to enable widows to rediscover themselves and realize their true power.

She wrote this book for those dear ones.

She can be reached on her blog or at miraclecor@aol.com.

Made in United States
North Haven, CT
29 August 2022

23404875R00035